THE SHAPE OF MY
COUNTRY

The Shape of my Country

*Selected poems
and extracts*

Tony Conran

ISBN: 0-86381-887-0

Cover design: Sian Parri

Published with the financial support
of the Welsh Books Council

First published in 2004 by
Gwasg Carreg Gwalch, 12 Iard yr Orsaf, Llanrwst,
Wales LL26 0EH
℡ 01492 642031   🖷 01492 641502
✆ books@carreg-gwalch.co.uk   website: www.carreg-gwalch.co.uk

READING A COUNTRY

A view of
The Shape of My Country
by Tony Conran

A country is shaped as much by its literature as by its maps. 'Imagining' the nation has become a fashionable way of speaking of culture and nationality. Visual art, music, drama, film, all forms of art and literature, make national cultures. Poems, because they are a distilled performance of and in words, present and represent identities with a special force of their own. This volume of poetry explores the history and identity of Wales in a geographical, social, personal and political sense. The collection brings periods of history, places and spaces, events and *la longue durée* to immediate attention. Identities are forged in the experience of reading or listening to the voices of and in the poems.

The collection makes a source book of Welsh history and culture, and the cross-referencing to other literatures, the visual arts and nature makes it an ideal curriculum resource for Welsh studies courses at all levels. The poems are a site for an argument in discussion of various points of view as well as a source of meditative individual reading.

The book benefits from listing the dates of original book publication and having fairly full notes on the poems. These will enable the references to the *Gododdin*, the *Aeneid* or the *Mabinogi* and some of the personal references to colleague poets and friends (I particularly love the poem 'Sisters') to be more fully understood. Perhaps in the future a critical edition could be usefully considered, with an introduction to the period and to Tony Conran's rôle and persona as a public poet. It could also discuss the rôle of poetry in both national languages in producing the nation. Such an edition could explore some of the enduring images in the poems, which have become a de-mythologised but refilled-with-meaning symbolism: Brân of the *Mabinogi*'s head at the Tower of London, for instance, becoming the icon of the United-disuniting Kingdom; Caernarfon Castle as the age-old symbol of a succession of imperialisms; and slate itself as the block from which identity is chipped. A millennial geological stratum worked by generations of human hands becomes an essence of nationality. In these poems the space called Wales is itself a palimpsest, an old manuscript always having to make way for new writing, but always left with traces of the old. Perhaps this future edition would also benefit from photographic reproductions of scenes and works of art, such as the paintings by Wilson and Turner which are the subjects of two poems; or of those ramparts of Caernarfon, or of the ever present magic birds such as the choughs.

Why publish this now? As the slates of Bethesda and Corris and Ffestiniog are being cemented on to the steel frame of the Wales Millennium Centre in Cardiff Bay yet another new cultural space is being re-made out of the remnants of old materials. Such is the subject of this book. It is a literary contribution to the re-making of the shape of Wales.

Dafydd Elis-Thomas

Acknowledgements

Sixteen of these poems are extracted from sections of *Castles*, twelve from *All Hallows* and four from *A Gwynedd Symphony* (Gomer Press). Others have been rewritten from work in *Formal Poems* (Christopher Davies Ltd) and *Poems 1951-67* (Deiniol Press), and three are collected in *Eros proposes a toast* (Seren Books). Of the remainder, 'Sarn' has appeared in *Planet*, 'Voyage to the Underworld' in *The New Welsh Review* and 'Ar y maes' (the Welsh original) in *Taliesin*.

I am very grateful to Dafydd Elis-Thomas for writing the foreword and for his helpful suggestions as to how the book could be improved, including the addition of notes. I was in two minds about this because poetry-readers are said not to like notes, but *The Shape of my Country* was compiled at least partly for Welsh people and incomers who don't know much about Wales and her history, to make them feel it as a living place and a place to feel at home in; and the poems don't always work if you don't know what they're talking about. There are notes and notes, of course. Having decided to include them, I wanted to make them interesting and on occasion controversial: for there's certainly no point in being boring. If the book is ever used (as Dafydd Elis-Thomas suggests) as a pedagogic resource, the notes might be useful to stimulate and direct discussion.

I want my poetry to belong to Wales, to speak of Wales and to Wales as itself: a multi-cultural community, a nation in its own right. I want it to play its part in countering the sense that Wales is only a rather disadvantaged part of Britain.

I would also like to say thank-you to Mrs Verena Davies for permission to use a reproduction of Paul Davies's glass mosaic *Baltic Republic/Heraldic Wales* as a banner on the cover. It makes a point of its own and my book would be a lot poorer without it.

Contents

III. Awakening and Defeat

IV. What to do?

Map into heraldry

It is time to make shapes of my country.
Block them with hardboard,
Planks, bits and pieces.
Glue them, tack them down.

It is time we recognised that that shape
Had a future.
Make your templates brash
With the red and the gold.

It is time for the shape of Wales
To have a future.
Hoist it up with bravado
So the cock Wales can crow.

I

CELTS

Lleyn

I have trudged this ancient land,
Sand-dunes older than Christ,
Fortifications of Mabinogi gods.

At every turn of the road
Shaman or saint
Holds me with some quirk of light.

Clynnog the great church
Gathers me like a pilgrim.
Silence round sacred wells.

Fern in the tumbled walls
And thorn hedges
Earth-red with winter.

To Llanaelhaiarn in the cup of the hills,
Under the cairns
Of burials older than my people . . .

Orwig

Shepherds, raw-faced from the wind
Banter in guttural Welsh.

They've been here so long, they look native.

But sheep are invaders too.
Until the eighteenth century
Round here was beef country.

'Orwig, lord of Gwynedd, giver of cattle . . . '

But even Orwig, who built the dry-stone cities,
Kraals that we call hillforts

– Even Orwig and his Welsh –
Invaded through the gaps

A dolmen-littered, alien land . . .
A folk that piled cairns, raised henges

And had (in their turn) invaded
Tundra,
          Glaciers . . .

Castell Dinas Brân

Brân, the Mabinogi giant,
is also Welsh for crow

But Brân isn't here. Crows,
Caretakers, squabble loudly
In the encircling scrub. Brân
Whom no house could hold, the Crow King
Brân is dead.

And yet I suppose of all gods
The dead divinity of this hill fort
Is my people's home. Both grandfathers
Hatched within five miles of here,
And over there
Along the gaps of Offa's Dyke
My Uncle Jesse farmed. Brân's fledglings
Or foster-chicks, the lot of us . . .
Caw caw, say I.

        It was poison
Finished Brân. We were told,
'Cut off my head. Take it,
It will talk to you.
The dancing civilization of the Crow
Will entice you. You'll dance,
You'll do love's music. Hundreds of blood years
You'll walk in the Crow's dream. In Gwales.
In the unrememberable lands –

Until one door is opened,
One latch pushed open.
It will be obvious, which door.
It will bring memories.

And wherever you are
– Gwales or Dinas Brân –
Must be left to the crows. High curtains.
Marriages. Children. Take my head.
It will not talk to you.
Dig it a deep hole in London,
Under the White Tower in London –
A hole for the Crow. That is success.
That is my will for you.
For unity's sake.
For Britain.'

Caw caw, say I –
Old crow.
Old carrion crow.

Giants

Up the sharp scree, up the lace alb
Of the hill, stepping
Where disks of rhyolite chink,
Up to the bleached skeleton
Of a hill-fort, laid out
On a limb of Yr Eifl
Under the running cloud.

Tre'r Ceiri we call it, town of giants.

Really, the giants are us,
Denizens larger than life
Of the erected scree. While we live
Each of these cauldrons of dry stone
Is capped like a kraal. Smoke
Twists its way through birch bark.
Moans of oxen hang round us like mist.

While we live, these parapets stand.

Cashel or rath, hillforts of
Dry stone or earth ramparts,
Clan homes, gathering places,
Shrines of the gods. Are our hearts
Littered here, is this where
The bones gasp and tear themselves in parturition
Among the starry tormentil
When we are brought forth – giants
And whole men, women whole as day . . .

Sarn

Pylons, six-armed, march the Roman road.

From Canovium on Conwy
To Segontium on Seint
There was a sarn. A road.

Gingerly, from stream valley
To dip in the rocks
To stream valley –

Afon Roe, Afon Tafolog,
Then across the foothills

Down Afon Anafon, to
Cross the Ogwen
into Armona –

Gingerly, for the terrain
Forbad straight lines,
The arterial sarn

Gave Venedotia
Four hundred years
Its Roman blooding.

Penmon

A stone cross stands in a field.
Headland calls over to headland.

Bright rock, bright sea. The grey
And glittering sand, the gulls.

A small, old, hunchbacked shepherd
Stands in the windy grass.

Chiselled, scooped out from the living stone
Convolutions that in death wear shallow.

Now headland calls, gulls call, sea,
Grey rock. Sunlight summons mankind to the sand.

Stone cross, tidy and dark and small,
Like a spent sun, stands in the windy shadow.

The simple country

I am O Conaráin, the poet.
I trudge a Merthyr street
At midnight. Deep snow sluices my footfall.

Once when I was in love, I stayed in that
Glazed-brick Victorian house.
Now I look up at the leaded windows,

Bemused they're not lit – in my day
We'd be talking
Politics or sex, till morning.

I'd been there one drugged week of love
When nothing but snow happened,
Nothing, yet it seemed to uncreate

The complex world, making all simple.
Now the windows are blank
With the dead sadness of a slum.

I think of the nothing,
The white body of a girl,
Nothing, and the six days of snow.

Narrator

Down the white street
One crouches
In the Gothic darkness of a doorway.

Poet

It's a cold night.

Stranger

Cold can't hurt me, Saxon,
And you are dreaming. I come
To meet you this New Year.

Poet

Who astonishes
The waste nostalgia of my dream
And claims such power to know me?

Stranger

Dewi I'm called.
While sin yet tempted me, Mynyw
I held as bishop, though more fit

To mourn my days in penance
On a bare rock shared by the gulls
Than bind and loose, by Christ entrusted.

Now, by God's grace, prayer reaches me
From Wales – your country as well,
Saxon –

Poet

Father, England is dying.
Out of the sprawl of that death
How shall Wales be saved?

Dewi

While I lived on the drowning earth,
Here, in this Island of the Mighty,
I knew magnates, ambitious men,

Magicians that tempted us to folly.
I knew their devils, just as you,
Their lusts, superstitions,

Idolatries of clay and self.
In God's grace we went, a handful,
To follow the Baptist to the wastes,

Laughed at – mourned by our brothers –
Exiles in our own land, wild geese
Migrating over the mind's ocean.

It was not easy saving the soul alive,
Winging the seas to the simple country
Beyond the stars, nearer than bone!

But look, with our salvation
A thousand years were freed of false gods,
Imps and predatory Mothers thwarted.

Hearts had air to breathe, lived under stars.

Poet

Father, simplicities wither.
In dank ground
Imagination rots.

A millennium won by you
Wales called her soul her own
Though prince and sovereignty both perished.

But now political weakness wastes
The seed. Unborn generations
Have no vision, and must die.

Dewi

Look over Dowlais.
Wind freshens, snowclouds roll
Like huge breakers towards us.

Sea monsters crowd the heart,
Rage through gap and crevice,
Chasten its fibres, bleach with salt.

I know them, and I tell you, Saxon,
Unless soul wings out against the sea,
The wild sea, shunning comfort,

No trust or innocence alive
Can save this people, who clutch
At reliquaries and household gods.

Poet (as Dewi moves away)

Bless your people. Father,
As you go,
Pray for us,

Your people who live in Wales.
Let spring come
With its old innocence

After this winter,
This wasting of us –
Water-carrier, grant us spring!

Choughs

Brân goesgoch, Brân Arthur –
Choughs tumble along the air.
There is more music in them.

Three choughs juggle with the wind.
Red-legged crows of Arthur,
They have the tune of it.

Choughs tumble below the fort.
They have the secret.
They are serious clowns.

Hook-mouth, they greet us.
They have messages for Lleu
Deft of hand; spells for Gwydion.

> And Marged looked up at the derelict roof. 'What's that?'
> she said, 'There!' Tucked in the beams of the quarry shed,
> dark and untidy, a chough's nest. As we stared at it, the
> silhouette of a curved beak, tense with the knowledge of us.

> That was round the next limb of Yr Eifl, in Nant Gwrtheyrn,
> in the Vale of Vortigern who had let the Saxons settle in
> Britain. Legend says it was under these cliffs he died.

Black choughs sound in the wind.
They are serious clowns.
They have messages.

Gwŷr a aeth Gatraeth

Men went to Catraeth – Aneirin

'Poets of the world
Judge the brave.' Did he say
Judge? That severe man
At the rock, the cashel
Of the Otadini,

Embro, Auld Reekie,
Caer Eidin – as they drank
The blue mead, as they
Jostled for the tidbits
– This young warrior and that –

Along the barbecues, men
Turning the spits
With the touch of mechanics,
The far-sighted charisma
Of men doing women's work –

The ritual speech
Of Hell's Angels
Out on a binge,
Commandoes in the sobering
Proximity of meat.

(Jessed peregrines strutted
Round the hearths, scuttered
Like hens, and the bitches
Nuzzled the palm, growled
For the oozing bone . . .)

Food for the crows
At Catterick, the eagles
Grey-hatted over
Yorkshire streams,
The timid wolves.

Trippers to Aberffraw
for Ray and Els

The village awkwardly pretends not to know
What violence was done here, or what craft
Intricate as Kells, was etched into the blood.

Falcon lord . . . head like a thrusting wolf . . .
White-as-millrace face of a girl

Litigations brilliant in verses
Of a grey court on the rocks hung over foam
Where London ambassadors heard all night
The cold Brythonic of curlews; or a young lad
Watched Sir Cormorant periscope for fishes –

The village awkwardly ignores it. Cottages
Of an undressed and barbarous stone, bestrode
By yellow Nonconformity like a slag tip

Where all the people seem somehow defective –
Lack leg or nose, or lisp, or quietly
Wander off, six months in the year, and no one knows.

The fourteenth-century Anglican church
Confides to itself a delegated past.

* * *

Geology forgets. The dunes grow big by night.
Curlews are crying from the salt profit
Of many moons. Sand's no legend-teller.

But the brilliant antiquity of the gold sun
Has summoned from this blown-about earth
A thousand flowers – tabby-faced pansies, bee
Orchis, succulents. Moonworts spike in the slack.
Though the light's a deal more ancient even than here,
Nothing – not even the sun – is as old as now.

* * *

You're off to Aberffraw? Curlews like Welsh bards
Will worry that such as you
Have come unmourningly
Glib as thieves' torches
Into their brittle Egypt of rock graves.

You reach the gold antiquity itself
Who ride your humping scooter to the sand
And lay out four slim legs for the sun to sign
And an idle toehold take of a tuft of grass,
Trickle and trickle fine fingerfuls of sand

Till the generous day leads home.

* * *

A red sky, boats like dried skulls, aground
        In scattered grey handfuls;
    Vociferously seagulls
    Cluster, hover round their hulls.

This village has come, somehow, all our glib
      Lies to disallow,
   Not free to be Aberffraw
   Names our sickness to us now.

* * *

I cannot face the eyes of here
Nor see along the sight of now.
I cannot night and day both focus,
Cold curlew cry and ramshackle town.

Insidiously the Princes wait
In grey-backed clusters calling of war.
Meanwhile your fingers in the idle sand
Trickle through peace, pain no more.

II

CONQUEST

Hillfort and Castle

A castle is a wedge in the soul.

The Earl had purchase from it,
Leverage
Like a pair of forks back to back
To divide
The warm belonging root of us.

I climb now to the Earl's opposite.

Hillfort rubble brakes the gliding eye
As it dives to the stream's cut,
Village and coastal plain. Beyond that,
Traeth Lafan's wettening sands
That led to Anglesey before the Bridge.

Here was a manifest destiny, a Holy Land's
Gate, Pillar of Hercules . . .

                    Down there
Like a child's near-perfect sandcastle
A tiny motte hides between cottages.

The Wedge, like a snake's tongue,
Flickered and moved on.

The Earl and the trees

'Clear the trees first,' said the Earl. 'No point
In giving 'em shelter.'
The first nail driven in.

The crying root wrenched free.
Whey-faced dirt heaped to a hill.
The forest scooped out.

Naked shoulders bit with an axe.
Thighs pushed the shovelling blade.
The first stake.

'I keep this motte,' said the Earl.
'The bare tump asserts me.
I keep this land.' But he didn't.

Much later, the towers built of jagged stone,
The drawn teeth of the land.
Cattle move through the water meads.

The trees are tamed. Sewage farm,
Stone village, visitors.
Afon Lleiniog drains good ground.

Where will the trees, the tattering trees
Go now, poor things?
In this winter for them, where will they hide?

In the Earl's tump, of course. They tower,
They tower and break. Their roots,
Their roots step in the hill.

And in the tower the cracks
Are the rhythm of rooting.
The walls lean out like a tree.

Counting song

In the soul. But first, in the soil.

Destructible wood and stone
Of the castle-builders. Lands
By compulsory purchase
(Or otherwise) appropriated
To service castles. Monasteries
By the grace of God
Moved up river. Whole townlands
Picked, dusted and re-potted
The other end of the world.

In the soil. But second, in the coffers.

Destructible writs, great seals
Dangling. Sheriffs,
Law-courts, officers
For the registration of fair
Trading. The quiet ways
Of simony and graft. The King's Peace
Stealing in on you
Like a mist over water-meadows.

In the coffers. But third, in the belly.

In the belly of compassion
The children hungry. In the belly
Of anger, fat cats of the King.
Destructible devils
Out of the corner of eyes.

In the belly. But fourth, in the prophecies.

Caves I can hear
Arthur's heart in the stone.
Mad Sweeney talks to the birds.

In the prophecies. But fifth, in the wastes.

Keep

But they are prisons too. Owain the red
For the mere accident of brotherhood
Kept at Dolbadarn.

Keep and kept. All poor claimants
To be suppressed, those worth the keeping
Held in the dungeon walls.

Flung in. If you broke a leg
Down the eight-foot gap
What's that between friends?

O castle my mother, womb
Of the aspiration in me,
To what springtime do you bear me?

Out of the belly of war
Protect me, mother. Pussy-willows
Fleck the rock with gold.

I can hear the mewing hawks
Climb on the air. Then the din
Of siegecraft, wood on rock,

Stone on rock, clang of iron
Wrenching, blundering.
Men scream in broad daylight.

Out of the belly of war
Protect me, mother. Ecstasy
Flecks the grey rock like sunshine.

At Dolwyddelan

I hear them call, ' . . . *wedi marw*' –
Up to the high keep on the hill.
Llywelyn is dead in the south.
I look through the watcher's eyes.

Through this arrow chink
Consternation of centuries
Is jagged as fork lightning.
I stare with the eyes of a young boy

Terror of death, dreariness
Of all my own deaths, my father's
Heart rasping to a close, Vic Neep
Daubing till the tumour dried his mind . . .

My sight shrivels. I turn to run.
Dreariness reaching back.
Procession of all my friends
Into that cry in the dawn –

The procession of my people
Calling up to me for seven centuries
As the Cilmeri raven
Wheels on the wing towards Dafydd in Dolbadarn.

The bulls

– Come, Dun Cow of Einion,
Stray-horns, Speckle o' the lake,
And Dodin the polled,
Up, come home.

Silences filled
With the moans and confabulations
Of cattle,
Rumours of great bulls . . .

Disappearances cluster like bees.
Castell y Bere
Lies low on its mound.

No, it was here, not Cilmeri,
Not by the Irfon at Builth,
Wales drained like brown blood into peat.

The last bull-protector of Britain,
The last Princeps Gwaliae
Defended his corner. Fled.

Feckless Dafydd in the April storm
Took to his heels
As the curtain tumbled,

As the stage curtain collapsed.

Bulls of the legions, in my lord's parks
Collected from the open woods like deer,
Chillingham, Vaynol –

Good for nothing now but to be wild,
Or remind us, like a zoo,
Of the bull-phantoms of Britain –

Come, Dun Bull, Pale Bull o' springtime,
Brown Puckerthroat, old Greyskin,
And Speckle, Maelgwn's bull –
Up, come home!

The bulls of sovereignty
Shall they come back to us,
Wild phantoms of Wales?

And the tall cows, shall they
By the lakes
Calve white, with perked red ears?

Gruffydd ab yr Ynad Coch

remembers his great lament for the Last Prince,
and the Conquest of Wales ca. 1300

Now peace, uneasy with treason, cometh
      Like an English conceit.
   Poetry I've known once
   Equal to huge occasion.

Occasion I howled the very Sabbath
      Of evil advancing,
   Occasion of eloquence,
   Of Apocalypse greeting

Greeting the sun darkened, the welkin
      Ravenous with eagles,
   Great lords upon battlefields
   And their big bones left naked.

Naked now the tradition, a gift bare
      Dug with their bones in dust,
   Penitence for the old craft
   And dearth of high occasion.

Occasion was, and is not. The havoc
      In the heart was piteous.
   He's a fool sounds the Trump twice
   With sour fondling of metres!

Caernarfon across brown fields

This is where empire begins.
It's the dragon's tooth.

Polygonal towers, faces
Of vertical shadow and light
Like long gem-crystals.

Patterning of tower and wall
With bands of coloured stone.

Three stone eagles face the sea.

– Such walls, such towers
Curtain under the eagles
Byzantium the Second Rome . . .

And whose idea was it, grubbing up
Tubers of a third
To sprout in these hills?
Which *Wledig*, Macsen or Cystennin,
Caesar Longshanks, plaudited
Imperator of the Brits . . .

Empire. That's what
Bites into these brown fields,
Rears over the trees
Into white air. Who set it
Ticking away like a bomb
Weeks, years, millennia?

Death to castles

It is terrible the revenge we take on castles,
Burn everything that burns, strip the lead roof.

Towers hang slipshod as we play King Kong,
Throw buttresses into the sea, tear curtain-walls like paper.

But rock calls to rock. Spleenworts
Star dark crevices. Stonecrop

Wanders the old mortar.
Lichens dye in rings.

Soon the trees will come. Primroses
And violets huddle by the stumpy wall.

And before this weapon becomes what it always was
– Geology and the processes of soil –

Before this folly inches like a scree
And slips utterly to ground,

Alys, aged six, turns cartwheels in the court,
Enfys, aged four, sings out from two-foot walls.

Ruin

Under sentence
The past exerts itself,
Resists shrinkage.

Though continually it slips,
Lets go of its space
(– How small these ancients are! –)
Yet here is a castle.
Dinosaur ribs
Elbowing out from the rock.

It takes all the energy that went into
Castles – dinosaurs –
Even to salvage this much being big

Where neither key nor signature
Scavenge, nor tell-tale nor anti-body
Diminish to the dust . . .

Even to stay put
As the structure moves into its future –

It takes the Earl's energy –
Tyrannosaurus Rex –
Even to dawdle you down like a wino
Onto its sloping laund.

Kidwelly castle

Donnes of Kidwelly, Herberts of Raglan,
Vaughans of Tretower . . . The marcher lords
Read like a preview of the metaphysicals.

Their castles are two-way. Talons
Reach into Wales, valley and farm,
Pasture and cabin. But they are homes too,
Stocks, studs, launching platforms
To London. Cadwaladr's
Red Dragon, Henry's flag
At Bosworth, standard of the last
Legendary British king. He used it
For his Union Jack.

Which great house
In those Welsh wars, Wars of the Roses,
Would do the act of Brân, bury its head
Under the London tump, for Britain,
For the unity of Britain?

Gwynedd's a subcontinent,
Gives no sufficient vantage. Castles there
Are about conquest. Independence
Attempted or overthrown. Dolbadarn
And eagled Caernarfon's loosed *imperium* –
The different scale tells all.

But when I kidnapped Chris Meredith to take me
To Kidwelly's half moon, my eyes pricked.
This was a home. For centuries they'd beavered,
Extended, modernised. The anxiety
Of property developers: would the market
Take it? Would that barbican

Do the trick? Was the new oven
Too far from the hall?

It made me think I'd left my glasses behind –
Poor Chris had to go back and look! No, no,
It was my Gwynedd eyes seeing Wales,
The castles of Wales, for the first time.

I had walked through the Himalayas into Asia.

The mordant

Seven hundred years
(But an old splendour
Dies hard)
Generosity, courage,

Quicksilver dispositions
Geared to a mainly
Genealogical
Salvation.

A man's root
Going down
To the rich loam –
The mordant

That fixed him like a dye,
Giving him covenant
And right to be lamented
In formal *marwnadau*.

That's all gone.
The great lords,
Father to son,
Changed pretty quickly

To English.
And as Siôn Cent
Might say,
'Where are they now?' –

Mae'r siwrnai i Loegr?
Mae'r swyddau mawr, os haeddir?
Practice for adolescent odes.
Gone to the wall.

Recusant

Fr. William Dai says mass on the Little Orme

For maids and farm labourers
Of Uwch Dulas, his cwmwd,
For wives and tradesfolk,
He offers it,

For the lost parishes of Creuddyn –
Llangystennin, Llanrhos, and high
On the table of the Orme,
Llandudno.

Westward to Seiriol's island,
Penmon, and his place of death . . .

And again his thought widens. Gwilym
From a family of harpers,
Telynorion, gives hostage
For them –

For cyweirdant and tyniad,
For variety of plucking,
For the twenty-four measures
Caniad and gosteg –

Being part of the mirroring
Of God's love
In the order of Wales,
Y Drych Cristianogol –

All the rough and tumble
Of minstrels, and the prosody
Free and intricate
As the growth of an oak.

It's down on its uppers, that Wales!
The patrons gone whoring
Like the newfangled bishops
After strange gods . . .

But wider, wider, for all Gwynedd,
For Britain, Christendom
And everywhere, men and women,
He offers the host. The hostage of time.

III

AWAKENING AND DEFEAT

The Awakening

From the arrogant stock
What then?
Saints, hymnwriters,
Ministers,

Preachers of prodigious sermons,
Revivals, Pantycelyn
And the yearning
Lifting like mist

Below Snowdon . . .
And still
The pride not to be English,
Not to be this or that,

Dividing Bethesda
From Seion
At the same end
Of the same village.

Zion

for Paul Davies, landscape artist

The innocent silver sea
Must learn to breathe,
Run on graven beaches,
Knuckle a cliff –

Must acknowledge the tricksy air,
The squirts of cloud.
Green hovers into fields.
Mist thins the world.

The Wales you made at Aber Alaw
In a rockgarden of wildlings
Climbs out of the night.

It is starry, it is Ephrath.

It is where Ann listened at Dolwar
To wassail of Methodists
On their wild travels.

It is Llanddewi-Brefi, a raised
Earth, a pulpit
For a blackbird or a saint.

It is Zion, it is clear water.

Enclosure act

Wilson's painting, *Speculum Dianae*

Tranquillity round the tower Dolbadarn,
The violence mummified
In the rich consciousness, but candid
As a pearl, as a lamp to pure thought.

The wand of the Grand Style he waved at it,
Put framing arbours, made the rounded lake Peris
Speculum Dianae, mirror of the moon.

And at the back Mount Snowdon –
Like the boundary of a fencing-in
Privatised
By the crachach, the posh gods.

Diploma piece

But Turner's prospecting eye
Digs into wild air.
Dolbadarn's an alembic of fantasy.

All's chemical – intractable
Bed of the glacier, block scree
And the clawed litter of cliffs

No less than breeze or cloud.
Marketable intimations
Uncrumple from his paint.

The little Cockney stands at the ford.
He launches the bolt of commodity
Deadly down the slatey stream.

And as the quarries dismantle the hills
And the chinking slates
Roof half the world,

Turner leaves at the Academy
'Dolbadarn' – a visiting card.

When Turner was elected an R.A. he gave the Academy a picture of Dolbadarn castle as his diploma piece.

Becca at the gates

You saw them shouting at Efail-Wen,
Preseli men round Mynachlog-ddu,
Swains of Llangolman and Maenclochog,
Farmhands, greybacks of Llandysilio –

You saw the wrath of Twm Carnabwth
The house-in-a-night man, who put stones
Round a hearth, a roof and a chimney
And a good fire alight by morning.

Gunfire and horsehooves in the darkness
And you saw Rebecca at the gate –
Red petticoats over ploughman's boots,
Bonnets and shawls, tall hats of women.

You were at the hosting at St Clears
Blackfaced on steeds round about Pwll Trap.
You saw the old bent Becca hobbling
Up to the gate, stooped on a thorn stick.

You saw the stick feel in front of her.
'Daughters, there's something put up here
Across the road, I cannot go on.'
Hundreds shouted, 'Mother, what is it?'

Nothing should bar your path, old Mother –
Not a great gate, nor bolted custom,
Nor opportunities taken away,
The theft that is wealth, or dumb respect.

You were with wassailers by moonlight
On familiar ground, under the stars.
Her cry rang out: 'Children, off with it,
Break the gate down, it's no business here.'

Stanzas of the graves

The black rain of gorse mountain
Seethes on the carved slate curtain,
The gravestone of Cynddylan.

After the muck and profit
And cattle banged to market
Rhydderch the sly lies quiet.

Grey urn instead of tankard
Brims over in this boneyard
For Evan Hael the drunkard.

Between scree and riverbed
Stands a blue slate at the head
Of the tireless Ednyfed.

After pomp and high office
Root and frost crack the surface
Of the tomb of Dafydd Prys.

Young and old, foolish and wise,
The graves blink at the sunrise
One by one, with hollow eyes.

Slate door-stop

A smug Victorian
Bureau, a tall
Paterfamilias of a desk
By the parlour wall,

Ornate with fan, fluting,
Circle and square,
Great knobs on the drawers (only
Half still there) –

Rubbished in my garden
A slate block
Carved by a quarryman
For a door-stop.

Folk art of an industrial world
Whose detritus we are,
The lost America of Wales
– Black dust, blue scar –

All the stripes and star of it –
Men perched like gulls
Along the sharp contours.
Pocketfuls

Of humanity
Thrown like seed.
Terraces round the treeless hill
Ropes of brown beads.

Gellionnen, Rhiwlas, Fochriw, Rhosgadfan –
The bloom of rock
Erupting into the ages of blood on the grass . . .
And with it, this block

Of dark slate, carved in a quarryman's hut
And smug with the pride
Of respectable men. – A grave stone
With learning inside.

Old man

In this quiet court in autumn, hither
And thither the leaves come
To the roll of frost's drum.

An old man sits empty-eyed, watching
The leaves drift and slide,
Rise and settle and subside.

'Jack, that you, Jack? Got me baccy?' – folk
Of the last century,
Jack and Huw, Nan, Eleri.

Lines on his parchment forehead, to ninety
Years of waste indented,
Name for witnesses the dead.

The old man sits empty-eyed, watching
The entrance to outside
Like a just jilted bride.

Voyage to the Underworld

Sic fatur lacrimans . . .
Aeneid, VI

At fourteen in the pit, in the mine
At Abertyssog.

The twin gates of sleep: one, rumoured
To be of common horn, gives easy
Passage to true dreams . . .

And me and Idris was working. And one time we got lost in
the colliery together for a few hours. We wandered into old
workings. We was lost for a spell there, me and Idris. We
was practically reared by one street next to one another,
down . . .

And at last we crowd on sail,
Glide under the Euboean coast by Cumae.
Prows are faced seaward, anchors bite
And make fast, and the curved poops
Fringe the litoral.

Our young men
Jump to it. Of my confrères,
Some try the flint veins
For the seeds of fire; others
The wild beasts' covert
Ravish for logs, and point
To water in uncovered rills . . .

But my piety is to make for the high summit
Where Apollo waits. The Sybil
In the pit of the years
Is a mare he must break and ride.

* * *

    Blaen Rhymni,
Entrance to the underworld.

There were still mines in the Valley then.
We came to the iron wheel
Between the trees, the turning roulette
Of the Sybil. We asked to go down.
No, it was not permitted. The golden bough
In the hands of a poet
Did not impress. But the colliers
Were coming up from their shift
To the polished air. Three black faces
Grinning like urchins in a king's robes
Posed over the barrier
To be snapped. Later
We saw them, fours and sixes,
Trudge archetypally
The brown lane to their wives.
Two of them waved.

It was seeing a film set –
Big John pushing the swing doors of a saloon
And the whisky
Trundling like a tall tram
Down the bar . . .

But they were people like us,
Spick and span from the newly installed
Coal-board baths.
No one sang
'Cwm Rhondda' or 'Llef'.

They tugged their forelocks.
We were tourists in Zion.
We grinned back.

* * *

Massive the rock's hewn out, a cavern,
A hundred wide mouths, a hundred gates
And as many clanging voices
As the Sybil responds.

We came to the foyer. 'Ask,'
She said. 'Ask. The oracle, look,
The oracle . . . ' And her voice
Trailed to convulsive silence, her face
Pocked with black tears.

It was time to pay our dues

. . . Will begin in one minute. Take your seats,
Ladies and gentlemen. The performance . . . '

. . . to Field Street. We was living in Ramsden Street, below
there. He went up to London or somewhere, from the pits
like. But we were very friendly up until the poor fellow
died. Cancer, I believe . . .

And gently my lips spoke. I remembered his question
In the desert of Wales, in the imploding
Emptiness of a dream:

'O what is coal
That so much blood should be upon it?'

And as I cried, like the pack of cards in *Alice*,
The whole caboodle –
    Pictures – soup kitchens
    The standing wheel – sunned colliers
    Country lanes
    Swans – pigeons – ponies put to grass
    Fiddles – jazz bands
    Federation
    Old women tearful in bare kitchens
    Hymns – hallelujas –

    Fell
Crashing at my feet.
'This way,' said the ghost

Till by the portals of sleep
We halted. The second gate
Gleamed in the emptying dusk,
Was elephant ivory. Through it
The lord of Shadows sends to the air
False dreams.

    Father Idris pushes me through.
I clamber out. Rejoin my confrères
At the campfire waiting the day.

'Landscape with moon, 1960'

As a churchyard has peace, because
In that place alone death has no power,

So to this territory of castles
– Dormant or extinct volcanoes of militarism –

Came one Neep, fugitive. From the deep
Arrow-slits his paintings look out.

As a churchyard has peace, because
In that place alone profit is powerless,

So to this country of waste-tips
A whole industrial revolution away from him

Already melding into the mountains, with a working-class
Crafty and demoralised and picturesque,

And an ignorant Taffia holding off ruin with one hand
And with the other making sure of its getaway –

Came, in due season, Neep. He centred us.
His cottage was the hub of North Wales.

Bethesda, Caernarfon, Rhosgadfan. Metropolitan
Of painters, poets, dramatists

In the two languages. They were extraordinary times.
And we who are thrown by the wheel's force

Into the darkness, like sparts from a forge
– All of us – confess that fire, that hub rotating

And confess the stillness there, the watching
Crouched by an arrow-slit, for the moon.

The sisters

Fifty years ago, the door hung open. Depredation
Of salt, emptiness, cold. Storm of the times

Bleached all the remnants. The jarred door
Had no room, no leverage to shut.

Souls drifted through it like leaves up an eddying street.
Children torn off in wisps to the gap of night.

A still-life of pitheads, embroidered with brown iron
Swayed in the raging tide like bladderwrack.

Gwales was crouched at odd holdfasts. War fleshed
Young men to the guns. Two sisters stirred

In the funnelling doorway. Then the blade of the door
Wagged in a gentler breeze. Its hinges mewed like gulls.

Two sisters on the holdfasts of Gwales, at Carmarthen
Tasted the far-off stars, the mission to bury the head.

* * *

And what of the holdfasts? In the nineteen-fifties
What were they? Two sisters, daughters of the manse,

Had the daily acquaintance of sanctity. A grandmother
Of Old Testament transparency, faith that moved

Not just mountains, but bankmanagers, tramps.
All around was the web of the chapel. Shudder of water

Biting their flesh with the Holy Ghost. Spluttering
In the absurd panic of baptism, given to Christ

By their father, dunking them in like sheep,
Like lambs that he carried with his arm

And the daily ordinariness of the household
With (just out of earshot) the hurrying flight

From the City of Destruction, the Slough of Despond
Criss-crossed by shocks of light, the growl of darkness.

As children they mocked and loved. It was holdfast.
The pure spring of it fizzed in their veins like champagne

And the language gathered them to itself. But still,
At the cinema, at the shop, the school,

The third door was ajar on them. Ripple and breeze
Creaked it back and to. Even their grandmother –

Even in the awareness they had of her – through *that* door
They looked, they felt the misery of what they were

And all that their people had been. The great head
Talked and laughed no more. It was a dead skull

In those seconds, the dancing civilization of the Crow
Did not entice them, the hundreds of blood years

Were as if they'd never existed, not love's music
Or their daily acquaintance with faith. A dead skull

And they'd to bury it, that's what those seconds told them,
Bury the Crow's head. Go with it, dumbly, to London.

* * *

How do I guess the process? – spoilt magic, bruises,
Relationships snubbed out, or dying, black-cored

Like a geranium wilting with rot . . . It's never easy
How the deep trenches of time bias or disturb

The momentary eddies that we live for.
The door was open. Nothing when you came, Non,

Offered to close it. You were the elder sister
Passionate and playful, moved with the current

Like a wild mink, a delicacy, a counterpoint
Of flutes. We wove our webs. You loved, mocked,

Were bruised. But the door in your time was open,
Nothing offered to hold you. You cried for air,

Air and the open world. You ran from a claustrophobia
That cornered you like toothache, no safer love

Could assuage or calm with home. Vision you were hunting –
Freedom where the meaningful and the heartfelt

Were as one. Wales held no vision then, except the head
Grey with death. When I visited you

Down sidewalks of Wimbledon, it was in the suburbs
Of your enterprise. Lovable and sudden

Like a young fox, you mocked its drabness.
But the wind bruised you on the sharp world –

Have you buried the head yet? In the dry rock of California
Thirty years on, you watch the blistered hills

From townlands resurfaced by the hour, disposable.
The webs of love trawl you, trawl you to this.

* * *

And the younger girl, Eirlys? – Snowdrop could anyone name
A pink scrap of a babe, and not mean by it

Under a lean sky, silence – purity – Spring's primal
Relation of living and holy –

Winter weighed by three petals – hanging force
Of faith's delicacy into the blizzard of time?

Not at all Eirlys. She was tropical as Jamaica,
Sardonic, a saturation of colours almost black –

A creature of warm interiors. It was a surprise
To see her outside, captured by humour or gossip

At shop doorways, or paddling through sallows
To meet small children off the bus. Yet

The name meant something. Was it
The empty focus of an ellipse, that pulls

A long comet towards the sun again? Abstraction
But in her orbits a condition of being?

It was the measure of her Resurrection.
Bulb in the brown earth. What people called her.

* * *

Both sisters had their courts. Clients gathered,
Friends, conspirators, those with a phrase to offer

Or a kindness, warmth or wildness, way of the world.
The magic of their Welshness was mediterranean,

Bright as seagulls. Lamplit palazzios
Where the twist and savour of a good story was king.

A taste of Gwales. The singing of Rhiannon's birds.
The Assembly of the Head these umpteen years.

But in Non's time, the door swung open, and she knew it.
Her court was at the rainbow's end,

Time-bound. Men of action, or men hesitant
To act. Women poised in the rigmaroles of doubt.

Time. Time. And the great space beyond. The shuffling
Seas sweeping you out through Aber Henfelin

To the gannet ways, the shark roads beyond Cape Clear.
But Eirlys, no. Oh yes, she knew the open door,

The dumbness of the head, the Crow's eye clouded.
But for her, in her time, the door was nodding shut,

Being defended. Vision in Gwales
As the poets sang, as the bards enacted

Dread imprecations. Flares went up. Prisons
Made gentle martyrs. There were prophecies of war.

And with it all, money. There was enough
To stay, to colonise the bare rock of dreams,

To home in on Bangor, make the language sprout again.
Teach. Act. Sometimes despair. But make home. Make home.

The tump under the White Tower could stay empty.
The Crow's head winked at us in our slum palaces.

IV

WHAT TO DO?

What now?

Lordship is gone. Sanctity
A failing investment,
Its credentials
Suspect.

What next? From the valleys
Of the South
Nye Bevan takes fire,
Prometheus

Of a Red Olympus like a ghost town,
Real fireworks
Terrible
In an English garden.

What next? Something must be done.
The Arts Council
Minces in teashops,
Talks

About striking a blow for Wales –
Five more minutes
In Welsh
On the Welsh BBC . . .

But surely the Welsh lord
Is like a phoenix,
A chick
Impossible to eradicate.

He has been prince,
Methodist minister,
Federation
Striker.

And now, must he not sprout
Even from these
Dirty
Ashes?

                    1958

A meritocracy?

An aristocracy of intellect
Could come – has come already

In a few displaced souls
From the lost generations.

Like all aristocracies
That of the intellect
Is a matter of breeding.

God spare us our lords
This time, that the English temptation,
The wolf with privy paw,

Take not away the sweetness
When the fire should rest,

As I have seen them go,
The third or fourth generation of the mind
Stolen from Wales.

Investiture, 1969

La connais-tu, Dafné, cette ancienne romance . . .
                                        Gérard de Nerval

The old tear-jerker, do you know it, Cymru,
At shattered root or under churchyard yew,
In unmade roads, or weedy in public gardens,
The sobstuff that always sprouts up new?

Towers do you recognise, and the Golden Gate,
And the sour fruit printed by your teeth,
And the deep cave, not open to visitors,
Where the drunk, beaten dragon-seed sleep?

The gods, they've come back! London's pretty boy
Virginal and neat, fresh as a frilled lettuce,
Kneels to his Dam! World shudders with prophecy!

O raddled Britannia still sucking her dream!
O fort of Constantine, functional yet!
Ah, the police! Ah, benevolent military!

Over the top

Cymdeithas yr Iaith

Across the gathered churches –
Barbed wire
Like brown archipelagos –
Across the pitiful ditches
Of sobriety –

Across the minefields
Of good families –
Across the interior
Of wayward snipers –
Across bluffs . . .

Each precious unwrapping
Of the good sword,
The conscience saved
From rust –
Each bayonet.

Stepping it out –
Tumbling companies
In the hollow morning
Gathered
Like the bottom of a scree.

To ask for a bugle

from Euros Bowen, prifardd

A thick tapering trumpet,
A rhizome of bronze
In a dark forge moulded and twisted
In spiralling rounds.

A wide bloom opens from the root –
A crater of red
Like a lake of smouldering molten stone
Erupts from its bed –

At the thin snakelike mouthpiece
An oracle of death
Through the pursued lips, teeth, tongue,
Straitens its breath.

You know the horn I speak of,
Whose formal cry
Gives ecstasy; whose hot bray
Commands men die.

1969

Incomers

No, look how young
These ferns
Crowd the balconies!
They're kids like Juliet,
Young opportunists
In love. The next cold

Will weed them. Like goldcrests
A pretty plumage
Will draggle the stone.
Theirs is no survival
Against time, but
Every year's holocaust.

Anyway, nothing in these
Glaciated hills
Is old. A few thousand
Years marked the
Utmost genealogy,
Hereabouts, of life.

There are places, Tenerife,
Madeira, even Southern England,
Where life's coeval
With the rock. Deaths
Leapfrog each other, back
To the land's origin.

Not here. A mile-high chisel of ice
Erased all recent death.
Nothing's continuous
With what swam or sank

In this mudstone. Life-wise,
Gwynedd's a new land.

I can feel Snowdonia
Like a Klondyke hitching me
Upwind to gold –
A new country,
Settler's home.

In the untrodden light
Come travellers
– Pilgrims or refugees.

The young ones
Crowd their balconies.
At the next cold
Opportunists
Draggle the heart.

Refugee camp –
Or a quality of light
Drawing us inward . . .

Which is it?

Bill of lading

Specification. Country 133.
WALES / CYMRU. Oaks
On the quickening hillside
Sprouting.

Stag, owl and salmon
Reservists. Daffodil
Through the woodland
Sounding.

The two crisp languages
Pulling like sails
Our barge
Into open sea.

We had a future. Bilingual
Wales, a destination
And a tide
Turning.

Raymond Garlick

In the low low lands
Of Holland you built you
A boat, you built you
A replica of a tall
Ship, a Dutch brig
For the adventures of peace.

A Dutch brig
Called Wales. It was floating
– Look! – in the green and white
Peace. With four and twenty
Sailor-lads you could
Box it about the main.

What tethered it?
What stopped the tall
Dutch brig of Wales
From sailing in the timeless sea?

– How do you like it, sir? Castles?
County Schools? Referendum?

From sailing in the lowlands low . . .

Referendum 1979

It was a day and it was a night.

In Llansteffan, never such a day
For seven hundred years.

Ianws the Yank, Raymond Cymro-Sais,
Cowered in history. The times
Flowed past like sheep.

O Conaráin in Arfon cowered.
'Keep your head down, boy,'
Said Gruffydd the beak's son.
'I've been here before.'

'Five hundred years . . . ' said Owain in Sycharth.

'A green force aborted,' said Ianws to Raymond.

'Ten years of boredom,' says Tripp in Caerdydd.

Belle View

And I watched outside the Belle View in Bangor
That night. The fairground in the A5,
Cars slowing for the tipsy crowdlets
Welling up from the College roads. I saw
John Dwy-Geiniog dance like a young goat
With a Union Jack on his shoulders. I saw
Cyril Halfpint climb through the rhetoric of ale
To the Four Branches of his joy. I saw
Englishmen already slipping the leash
Of what interest they had. I saw
The Blaid apologetic
For a nation foreclosed.

Caesar

Suddenly in the forum pomped
The hag Caesar crowned with laurels.
Eagles trundled to the last Imperialist War.
Falklands, albatross roads,
Marched them to glory.

We were in Galway then. Wary paudeens
Kept their usual distance.
I could hardly credit it.

But coming home
Under Caernarfon walls
Where empire began

(O castle my mother, womb
Of the aspiration in me,
To what springtime do you bear me?)

I saw the warmongering populace of England
Crowd on sail

As if it were normal, dismemberment or death
For queen and country, and not to complain
At the raggedness of hopes, the size of terror –

The hag Money taking the salute
Of the forty-three Welsh corpses
On board the Victory Victory O.

Elegy for the Welsh dead, in the Falkland Islands, 1982

> Gwŷr a aeth Gatraeth oedd ffraeth eu llu.
> Glasfedd eu hancwyn, a gwenwyn fu.
> > – *Y Gododdin* (6th century)

Men went to Catraeth, keen was their company.
They were fed on fresh mead, and it proved poison.

Men went to Catraeth. The luxury liner
For three weeks feasted them.
They remembered easy ovations,
Our boys, splendid in courage.
For three weeks the albatross roads,
Passwords of dolphin and petrel,
Practised their obedience,
Where the killer whales gathered,
Where the monotonous seas yelped.
Though they went to church with their standards
Raw death has them garnished.

Men went to Catraeth. The Malvinas
Of their destiny greeted them strangely.
Instead of affection there was coldness,
Splintering iron and the icy sea,
Mud and the wind's malevolent satire.
They stood nonplussed in the bomb's indictment.

Malcolm Wigley of Connah's Quay. Did his helm
Ride high in the war-line?
Did he drink enough mead for that journey?
The desolated shores of Tegeingl,
Did they pig this steel that destroyed him?
The Dee runs silent beside empty foundries.
The way of the wind and the rain is adamant.

Clifford Elley of Pontypridd. Doubtless he feasted.
He went to Catraeth with a bold heart.
He was used to valleys. The shadow held him.
The staff and the fasces of tribunes betrayed him.
With the oil of our virtue we have annointed
His head, in the presence of foes.

Phillip Sweet of Cwmbach. Was he shy before girls?
He exposes himself now to the hags, the glance
Of the loose-fleshed whores, the deaths
That congregate like gulls on garbage.
His sword flashed in the wastes of nightmare.

Russell Carlisle of Rhuthun. Men of the North
Mourn Rheged's son in the castellated vale.
His nodding charger neighed for the battle.
Uplifted hooves pawed at the lightning.
Now he lies down. Under the air he is dead.

Men went to Catraeth. Of the forty-three
Certainly Tony Jones of Carmarthen was brave.
What did it matter, steel in the heart?
Shrapnel is faithful now. His shroud is frost.

With the dawn men went. Those forty-three,
Gentlemen all, from the streets and byways of Wales,
Dragons of Aberdare, Denbigh and Neath –
Figment of empire, whore's honour, held them.
Forty-three at Catraeth died for our dregs.

Activist

Paul Davies, painter of maps of Wales

Maps were the wassail he took round.
He hawked them like a religion
From door to door, the lottery of faith.

'Will you sign?' Will you join this artwork –
Tie a knot here for the unemployed,
Come on board the Jubilee train?

His maps created an action committee, an affray.
We stood at Efail-wen before Thatcher
In our women's skirts, in the Falklands.

We were the very last unscheduled appearance of
Owain Glyndŵr. Not before time
We laid claim to the *bro* of summer stars.

A square of grey slate

presented to Pedro Perez Sarduy, Cuban poet, at the Wales-Cuba Resource Centre at the National Eisteddfod 1985 in Rhyl.

Days I have been wondering, Señor,
How I should speak:
The very language I use being wrong
For Eisteddfod week,

And yet I'm not satisfied
To mumble it glumly
As a mere *lingua franca*
Between Cuba and Cymru.

My tongue's my own, True Thomas says.
How then
Can I speak in the crowding name of all Welsh
Women and men

To offer you, Señor, the brotherhood
Of Welsh Wales?
How can I strike red fire from the very iron
Of our chains?

This morning early, I went to my rainy garden
Hoping to find
A messenger – perhaps a riddle
Of times out of mind –

A palimpsest of my people, a forgotten tryst
That I could keep
For them this Monday morning
Of Eisteddfod week.

There in the path was this square of grey slate.
Let that stone
Be my herald, I said, let its mute cry down the years
Atone

For my English. Let it speak
Where I cannot
Of the Welshness of Wales
Now, on this spot.

Men die here for stone. The ancient strata eroded
By rain, by frost,
Till the massif's a mere negative
Of what it was . . .

Señor, stone is the stuff of oppression
In this land.
Look, the conqueror's castles, Rhyddlan, Rhuthun, Denbigh
Still stand.

No one in Wales is untouched by rock.
Coal and slate
– Laid down before dinosaurs walked the world –
Dominate

Vast tracts of our industry, our past.
It was for stone
That the shanty-towns mushroomed
To chapel and home.

Rock was our vortex. Our working class
Was drilled from it.
Their dream and their discipline answered
The greed of the rich.

Strike. Lock-out. Depression.
Let this stone lip
Tell of those terrible years.
Now, slate-tip, coal-tip

Rear up like pyramids. Pharaoh and Israelite
Share
The memorial of the dump
Under wide air.

Welsh poets in love, Llywelyn Goch, Dafydd or Iolo,
Used to sing
Poems to thrush or tomtit, salmon or north wind
– Anything

Under the moon that moved, he'd make it
Ambassador,
Messenger, *llatai* for him, to travel
Straight to his girl's door

And tell her how much he loved her
And how much
He died, died for the sight of her,
Died for her touch.

Now therefore I command this square of grey slate
To go *llatai* for me
Through Westerlies and Trades
To the Carib Sea.

Go, little Fidelista of slate,
To the midmost
Of the Americas, where the plumes of royal palm
Mark Cuba's coast.

Go to the sugarcane fields, the rice paddies,
The orchards –
Go where the blacks once died like flies
As the cash flowed northwards.

And tell them, slateling, about our country,
This place of stone
At the edge of Capital's shadow
As the day comes on.

Wales

Wales is like perspective, it describes the space
Imagination is using. As in the inside-out
Perspective of Chinese silks,
The vanishing point
Is you.

Daughter of Becca, the gate's waiting.

You're faced with desolation and hope.

Pilgrim Way

> remembering Robin Reeves
> editor and mountaineer

A hesitant face, a man from the winds
Whose speciality was rock, and paths through rock,
Yet shaped like a stream bed in the trembling sands,
Weather, and gravity, lightning, dark . . .

A journalist must ride Time like a bronco
And the times were not good. Wales in '79
A depleted world, frighted of itself. Echoes
Of Cilmeri rubbished our leaf like acid rain.

Yet he had time, and the integrity of a pilgrim,
To saddle himself to the journey. The dirt road
To nationality out of tribal mayhem
Continually reaches dead end. As poetries fade,

He, whose speciality was rock, paths through rock,
Citizen of Tŷ Ddewi, unblocked the track.

Ar y maes

i Wynn Thomas

Ar faes y gwir, ar y cadfaes,
Gwelais y ddwy fyddin, clywais eu llefain
Yn y bore, yng ngolau niwlog y wawr:
Meddwn wrth fy ffrind, wrth y cerbydwr
Â'i law ysgafn ar yr awen, wrth y duw:
'Gyrra fi allan, Krishna, rhwng y lluoedd
Lle medraf weld y cyfeillion a garaf
Ar y ddwy ochr, y doethion
Sy'n barod nawr
I frwydro, ac i ladd ei gilydd.'

Felly gyrrodd Krishna'r cerbyd gwych allan
Ar y paith, at yr anialwch rhyngddynt.
Edrychais ar y ddwy linell,
Nid i'r gorllewin, nid i'r dwyrain,
Ond ar y ffiniau tu mewn,
Ar Ororau'r enaid.
Gwelais dadau fy nghenedl
A'u meibion yn sefyll yno i gyd.

Ar y naill linell, gwelais y Gymru
Sy'n dibynnu arni hi ei hun.
Gwelais fab yr ynad
A gwynodd am Lywelyn gynt,
Yn fud nawr wedi'r gwynt a'r glaw,
Gwelais Owain ffyrnig
Yn diflannu ac yn dod eto
Fel cledd allan o'i wain hir.
Gwelais y bardd o Fadog, brodor o'm bro,
Saunders a Gwenallt hefyd,
A Waldo, dyn yr heddwch

Ond gyda'i darian fry
Yn y blaen serennog.

Yng ngogoniant ei etholiad, Gwynfor
A welais. A gydag ef, mewn torf gymysg,
R.S. a Harri Webb a Tripp
A'r rhai eraill di-rif, bobl ddi-enw.

Ac ar yr ochr draw, gwelais Gymru
Yn ei breuddwyd Rhufeinig, y Gymru
Sydd ym Mhrydain, mewn ymerodraeth.
Gwelais Iolo, bardd coch y Fwyall,
Sef y Cwnstabl Hywel
Yng nghastell y brenin. Dafydd
A welais, a'i wallt
O ben ei chwaer; ond mewn brwydr,
Y mwyaf. Guto hefyd, yr henwr
A ddaeth yma o Ryfeloedd y Rhosynnau
A'i law ddall sy'n gryf mewn cad.
Roedd y Tuduriaid yno, a'u deddf
A thair canrif ar goll amdani.
Gwelais fy nhad, a'm taid o'r Waun
A llawer o'r hen gymdeithwyr,
Sosialwyr, fel Keir Hardie a Nye,
Ac athrawon a beirdd. Dylan oedd yno
A'i farwoldeb fel gwaywffon
Yn ei law . . . Talodd am ei fedd.
Wrth imi edrych, llifodd anobaith fy nghalon,
Galar ac anobaith am Gymru,
Am feistrolaethau'r wlad
Fydd yn darfod ar y maes hwn.

'Krishna,' ebe fi, 'mae'r ddwy linell yn torri
Fel briw trwy Gymru, trwy'n byd.
Rydym yn byw ar draws ffawt:

Mae toriad yn y ddaear
Dan ein sylfaen, dan y bryniau,
A gyfyd ac a egyr fel blodyn gwael
I'r wybren. Mae ffawt enfawr
Yn ein tynnu ar wahân,
Mewn dyffryn hollt mae'r arwyr
Yn sefyll fel dau glogwyn.

Gwych yw'r ddwy fyddin
A'u cwmnïau sêr fel llwybr
Trwy'r ffurfafen ddu;
Eithr rhyngddynt mae ffordd dagrau
A sianel i'r heli.

Dau gyfandir sy'n symud i ffwrdd
Dan ein traed. Nid ymladdwn
Ond i greu gwacter, i agor eigion.
Ac ynof innau, rhed yr heli
Rhyngof fi a'm calon. Tyf yn ddyfnach –
Ehangach yw'r môr chwerw o ddydd i ddydd.

Gan imi weld y Cymry, fy nghyfeillion
A'm cydwladwyr a ddaeth i'r maes hwn,
Difywyd yw f'aelodau. Syrthiaf.
Mae fy ngheg yn sych, fy nghorff yn crynu,
Mae'r bwa mawr yn cwympo o'm llaw –
Gandiva, bwa tanllyd y dychymyg.
Ni allaf sefyll. Krishna,
Yn erbyn y ddaear ei hun y brwydrwn.
Ni ragwelaf ddim ond drwg, ond cywilydd.
Nid oes ogoniant os briwaf fy ffrindiau,
Os lladdaf fy ngheraint yn aberth y gad.
Ni ddymunaf fuddugoliaeth na lles,
Nid oes eisiau arnaf gael teyrnas
Na'i mwynhau . . . O Janardana,

Symudwr eneidiau, os lladdwn y gwŷr hynny,
Daw drwg ohono. Gwell gennyf yn wir
Pe delent o hyd imi heb arfau
Ar y cadfaes, a lladdent fi yno!'

Fi oedd Arjwna, ar faes y frwydr,
Lleinw ei anobaith fi â galar:
Ei fwa a'i saethau a gwympodd o'm llaw.

Cododd ysbryd Krishna, dywedodd Duw
Wrthyf fi, wrth ei gyfaill:

'O ble y daw'r gwan-galondid hwn?
Ni wŷr y cryfion anobaith, Arjwna.
Am ŵr sy'n ŵr yn wir, nid yw'r hwn yn wiw.'

'Krishna, ni wnaf ymladd,' ebe fi.
Gwenodd Duw a dywedodd wrthyf:
'Mae dy ddagrau am y rhai y tu hwnt i ddagrau.
Ni alara'r doethion am y rhai sy'n byw
Nac am y meirwon ychwaith . . . '

Yn sydyn, ciliodd y breuddwyd
Wrth i Dduw siarad,
Wrth i Krishna ganu.
Toddodd i ffwrdd i'r gro,
I'r tywyll rhwng cerrig mân.
Diflannodd y cerbyd a'r cerbydwr
A'r ddau glogwyn o arwyr. Ni welais
Ond gwacter y goleuni
A sarnau hir y wawr.

On the battlefield

for Wynn Thomas

I saw, on the field of truth, the two armies,
I heard shouts in the misty dawn.

I said to my friend, the god,
The charioteer, his hand
Light on the reins –

'Drive me, Krishna, between the two hosts,
So that I may see, on each side,
The wise men that I love, who are now
Readying themselves to fight
And slaughter each other.'

So Krishna drove the bright chariot
On no man's land, on the prairie between them.
Neither east nor west were those warlines,
But on the soul's boundaries,
The Marches within us.

I saw the fathers of my nation
And their present-day heirs
Marshalled.

On this side, I saw
Wales look to itself as itself,
Llywelyn and fierce Owain, vanishing
And coming again, like a sword
From a long scabbard. I saw
Madog's poet, and Saunders,

Waldo the man of peace – his shield too
High in the starry front.

In his election's glory, Gwynfor
I saw. And with him
In a confused crowd
R.S. and Webb, John Tripp
And others numberless,
Not to be named.

On the other side, I saw
Wales in its Roman dream, Wales
In Britain, in empire. Brân, Macsen,
Eagles over Seiont, and Lord Axe –
Constable Hywel
In the castle of his king.
Dafydd I saw, his hair
Long like his sister's; but in battle
Not least. And Guto, the old man,
His blind hand strong in onslaught.
I saw the prophesied Tudors
And their Act, with the three
Centuries it lost us. I saw my father,
My grandfather from Chirk
And with him, comrades,
Keir Hardie and Nye,
Teachers and poets. Dylan –
His own death like a spear
In his hand – paid for his mead.

As I looked despair flooded me,
Grief and hopelessness
For the masteries of Wales
That on this field would end.

'Krishna,' I cried, 'nothing
Is for the good. The warlines
Cut like a wound through our world.
We live on a fault. The earth's broken
Under our bedrock, under
The towering hills, opens
Like a livid flower to the sky.
It's an enormity
Pulls us apart. Heroes
In the rift valley stand
Like two cliffs, armies
Splendid as companies of stars,
A path through the sky –
But between them there's a way of tears,
There's a widening channel
For the salt sea.
Under our feet continents are moving.
We fight only to make emptiness
And open an ocean.

For in me too, salt water runs.
Between me and my heart
Day by day, waste widens.
When I see my compatriots,
My friends here on the two lines,
My limbs sink lifeless. I stumble.
My mouth is dry, my whole body shudders,
And the bow of burning gold, *Gandiva*,
Falls from my hand. Krishna,
We are fighting against Earth itself.
I can only foresee evil
And desperate shame from it.
It's no glory to wound one's friends
Or slaughter relatives
In the holocaust of battle.

I can't wish victory or profit,
Nor do I covet a kingdom, to own
Or enjoy it. O Janardana,
Mover of souls,
If we fight, great evil
Shall come of it. Better if they found me
Unarmed and helpless
On the battlefield
And killed me!'

In the arena of war I was Arjuna.
His hopelessness filled me with grief.
His great bow clattered from my hand.
The spirit of Krishna arose,
He spoke to me.
God said to his friend,

'How comes this dejection, Arjuna?
In the hour of trial, strong men
Do not despair.'
'Krishna, I will not fight,' said I.

Then God smiled, and he said,

'Your tears are for those beyond tears.
Wise men do not mourn the living,
Neither do they grieve for the dead . . . '

But suddenly, as Krishna spoke,
As God was singing,
The dream escaped me,
                        melted,
Ran down into gravel
                        into the darkness
Between small stones.

Chariot and charioteer both
Vanished, and the two
Cliffs of heroes . . .

There was nothing to see
But an emptiness of light
And the long
Causeways of dawn.

Notes

*(Dates in brackets are of first book publication.
Lack of date implies newly published material.)*

Lleyn (1998). The peninsular of north-west Wales, beyond Caernarfon.

Orwig (1998). A Welsh name, meaning one of the Ordovicii, a Celtic tribe of eastern and northern Wales.

Castell Dinas Brân (1993). A hillfort and then a castle overlooking Llangollen. Brân, whose name means raven or crow, is thought to have been originally a local Celtic god. His story is told in the Second Branch of the *Mabinogion*. After his death in Ireland, his head was cut off and taken to an Otherworld on Gwales. Here it feasted with his followers till one of them opened a forbidden door facing Cornwall, when the head died and had to be taken to be buried in London, to protect Britain. I see this myth as an embodiment of the Welsh consciousness of the provisional nature of Welsh culture, in the last resort to be sacrificed for 'Britain'. The hunger for 'Britain' has eroded Welsh freedom of action for over a thousand years: it is time we got rid of it.

Giants (1993). Tre'r Ceiri (the giants' town) is a hillfort in Lleyn, still remarkably well preserved.

Sarn. Armona – Arfon; Venedotia – Gwynedd.

The Simple Country (1967). Dewi Sant – St David, patron saint of Wales, called the 'water-carrier' presumably because he baptised so many converts.

Penmon (1967). The ancient Celtic cross at Penmon used to stand in a field behind the monastery ruins but has since been moved into the church.

Choughs (1993). Lleu and Gwydion are characters in the Fourth Branch of the *Mabinogion*.

Gwŷr a aeth Gatraeth (1995). One of the earliest collections of Welsh poetry, *The Book of Aneirin*, is at least partly a sequence about a war-band collected by the chief of the Gododdin or Otadini, a tribe centred on Din Eidyn or Eiddyn (Edinburgh – Embro and Auld Reekie are later nicknames for the city). He trained and feasted them for a year, before they rode south to try and re-take Catraeth (Catterick in Yorkshire) from the Anglo-Saxons. They failed and all but one – the poet Aneirin – were killed. 'Poets of the world judge men of valour' is a quotation from this book and a classic statement of the function of heroic poetry.

Trippers to Aberffraw (1967). Aberffraw was the seat of the kings of Gwynedd and so of Llywelyn ap Gruffydd, Prince of Wales, till the Conquest of 1282. Sand dunes began to encroach on the area in the sixteenth century. Nothing is left but a cluster of dwellings above the sand-flat at the mouth of the Ffraw. Cardiff was made the capital of Wales in 1955, and in 1965 (the year before this sequence was finished) it became the seat of a new Quisling government called the Welsh Office, with some devolved powers responsible to a Secretary of State. Aberffraw, the old 'capital' of independent Wales, was as good a fly in the ointment of this arrangement as one could wish; though it is an uncomfortable, schizoid place, for a nationalist as much as a Britophile Welshman. No one really wants to revive the thuggery of the Welsh princess, and yet we can't as a people look them in the eye and say boo. One envies tourists who can take advantage of Aberffraw as a quiet bit of seaside without the 'falcon lord', the 'head like a thrusting wolf', breathing down their necks and prophesying war.

Hillfort and Castle (1993). The scene is Abergwyngregyn, at the mouth of the Menai Straits, a few miles to the east of Bangor. For the 'Earl' see the next poem.

The Earl and the trees (1993). The Earl of Chester, called Lupus (the Wolf), launched the first Norman invasion of north Wales. He made the motte at Abergwyngregyn and this one at Aberlleiniog, between Beaumaris and Penmon on Anglesey. He was ejected from Gwynedd by Gruffydd ap Cynon, whose successors ruled until the Edwardian conquest in 1282. The motte was re-fortified with a stone keep in the later middle ages.

Counting song (1993). Edward I, to build his fortified towns and castles, moved the original inhabitants of Beaumaris (Llanfaes) to Newborough on the other side of Anglesey, and the monastery at Conwy to a site several miles up river.

Keep (1993). Dolbadarn was a native Welsh castle near Llanberis. Rivalry between Welsh princes was often savage, because they were fostered by different (and ambitious) noble families as children. Llywelyn kept his brother Owain a prisoner in Dolbadarn for most of his life. The poem is deliberately impressionistic: it was in Edward I's castle at Conwy that prisoners were apparently dropped eight foot into the dungeon.

At Dolwyddelan (1993). Another native Welsh castle. I imagine myself there hearing of Llywelyn the Last Prince's death at Cilmeri near Builth in 1282. His brother Dafydd tried to continue resisting Edward I's conquest, first from Dolbadarn then from Castell y Bere in Merioneth. See the next poem.

The bulls (1998). The bulls' names are from the *Triads*.

Gruffydd ab yr Ynad Coch – Griffith, son of the red judge (1960). When Edward I destroyed Welsh independence by killing Llywelyn, Gruffydd ab yr Ynad Coch wrote an elegy for the prince, one of the greatest poems in the language, in which he saw the conquest in apocalyptic terms.

Caernarfon across brown fields (1993). Edward I (Longshanks) deliberately modelled Caernarfon castle on the walls of Constantinople and took care to accentuate the Roman associations of the place. Macsen and Cystennin are the Welsh forms of Maximus and Constantine, the names of Roman emperors associated with Britain. *Wledig* means a ruler. Caernarfon was a mighty stronghold, but even so it was probably more important as a document promulgating a new empire than as a military fortress.

Death to castles (1993).

Ruin (1993).

Kidwelly castle (1993). The Anglicised name is deliberate. Dolbadarn was a native Welsh castle, contrasting both with Edward's royal Caernarfon and the marcher lord's Kidwelly.

The mordant (1960). Siôn Cent, a Welsh 15th century poet who satirised the bards and their patrons. His sardonic lists remind one a bit of Villon. The Welsh quotations mean, 'Where are the trips to England? Where are the great jobs, if you're up to them?'

Recusant (1998). See *Sir William Dai: A Life of the Venerable William Davies, Catholic Martyr* by Patrick J. Crean (Catholic Truth Society, 1985). William Davies (or Dai) was from Uwch Dulas – where I was brought up as a boy – the area round what is now Colwyn Bay. He trained on the continent during

110

Elizabeth's persecution of Catholics, and after his return to Wales as a priest he and other Catholics founded a secret press in a cave on Rhiwledyn (the Little Orme) and produced the first book ever to be printed in Wales: *Y Drych Cristianogol*, 'The Christan Mirror'. He was finally martyred in Beaumaris.

William (Gwilym), Dai's grandfather was a famous *telynor* (harper). Welsh bardic harp music, extinct save for one partially deciphered MS, relied on a patterned alternation of chords on two harmonic centres, the *cyweirdant* (key-note or tuning string) and the *tyniad* (pulling out), which apparently varied according to the tuning. There were conventionally twenty-four 'measures' or patterns of such alternation to match the twenty-four metres of bardic poetry. *Caniad* (lit. a singing) and *gosteg* (usually translated 'prelude' but lit. a silencing) were large-scale compositions of this music. The ways the strings were plucked were also crucially important and systematized.

The Awakening (1960). The great Methodist 'revivals' of the eighteenth and nineteenth centuries formed a cultural revolution which changed Wales for ever, sweeping aside the old hierarchical social norms and giving Welsh people a new sense of their individual worth which stood them in good stead as they became the proletariat of the heavy industries – steelmaking, coal-mining, quarrying – that now began to transform the country. At the same time, however, much traditional 'folk' culture was lost, and the individualistic nature of the Awakening led to disunity and fission into separate sects.

Zion (1995). Ephrath – the region round Bethlehem, where Christ was born. Ann (Griffiths) the mystic and hymnwriter, before she was converted, used to listen to the Methodists singing through the countryside on their way to religious gatherings. When Dewi Sant *(St David)* preached at Llanddewi-Brefi the ground rose under his feet to give him a pulpit.

Enclosure act (1993). See next note.

Diploma piece (1993). Two great eighteenth-century artists, Wilson and Turner, in a period of intense class-struggle, painted Dolbadarn: Wilson, the master of the grand style – though he may have had other intentions as well – portrayed the values of the great squires, secure in the enclosure of the common land which they were pushing through with indecent haste. Turner, on the other hand, was the counterpart of Shelley, a painter of chemical change, of the age of storm and dynamic change. Turner is a prophet of bourgeois freedom, ultimately what he paints are the values of the free market, the winds of change. Dolbadarn, therefore, is part of the iconography of English art. When Turner was elected an R.A. it was a picture of Dolbadarn that he gave as his diploma piece. Neither Wilson nor Turner painted the castle realistically: both used it for ultimately ideological ends.

Becca at the gates (1995). Toll-gates were a major source of unrest in mid-nineteenth-century Wales, as they made movement of goods etc. prohibitively expensive and had a knock-on effect through the entire rural economy. Rioters calling themselves 'Daughters of Rebecca' in a spirit of high theatre would dress up in drag to tear down the gates that were taking away their livelihood. The first riot was at Efail-wen in West Wales in 1839, but the movement spread also to other regions. Each band of rioters had its own 'Rebecca', a leader dressed as an old mother who pretended she could not get through the gate till 'her' daughters tore it down. Twm Carnabwth (Thomas Rees) of Mynachlog-ddu in Pembrokeshire was at the riot at Efail-wen. It is said he had taken advantage of the traditional 'law' that if you were able to build yourself a house in one night and had a fire burning in the hearth by morning, you were allowed to keep it. The place-names in the poem are from Pembrokeshire and Carmarthenshire. 'Beca' or 'Becca' was the name of a group

112

of nationalist and left-wing artists associated with Paul Davies, and 'Becca at the gates' was the name of one of their exhibitions.

Stanzas of the graves (1967).

Slate door-stop (1987). Gellionnen and Fochriw are in the Glamorgan coal-field, celebrated by Gwenallt and Idris Davies respectively; Rhiwlas and Rhosgadfan (where the novelist Kate Roberts was brought up) are slate-quarrying villages in Gwynedd.

Old man (1967).

Voyage to the Underworld. As part of our production of Idris Davies's dramatic poem about the 1926 miners' strike, Jim Davies of Pontypool, Lesley Bowen and I visited Rhymney. We interviewed old miners and others about the strike and about Idris Davies himself. This sequence is partly a collage of those interviews with the passage in Virgil (*Aeneid* Bk. 6) where the Sybil leads Aeneas down to the world of the dead. Apollo is the god both of poetry and oracles, and therefore the Sybil's master.

'Landscape with moon, 1960' – the title of a painting by Victor Neep – (1993).

The sisters (1993). Holdfasts – the sucker-like organs which attach seaweeds to rocks. For the 'door', Gwales, the 'head' (of Brân) etc. see the note to 'Castell Dinas Brân' above. The younger sister's name, Eirlys, means 'snowdrop' in Welsh.

What now? (1960).

A meritocracy? (1960). My sequence, 'An Invocation of Angels', from which this section is taken, pinned its hopes on the creation of a new Welsh intelligentsia which, if it could be persuaded to stay in Wales, would take over the vacant leadership of the country and hopefully carry it to independence. I was accused, naturally, of elitism; nor did I know much about the stirring in Welsh Wales centred on poets like Saunders Lewis, Kitchener Davies and Waldo Williams. However, from the vantage of 2004, a lot of what I prayed for has in fact happened, and not least the revitalisation of Welsh youth. But whereas the Welsh-speaking intelligentsia *has* provided leadership – at least for its own linguistic community – on the whole the English has not, preferring a *trahison des clercs* and seeing its class-advantage only in the opportunities of British (i.e. English) middle-class existence. The result has been to split Wales from top to toe on linguistic grounds. A kind of tribalism has developed, in which the sense of a *gwlad*, a country of *Cymry* or compatriots, is being progressively undermined. *Iaith* (language) rather than *gwlad* has been the pre-occupation of both the Welsh intelligentsias, at least since the nineteen-seventies. The result, in the short term, has spelt some economic disadvantage for the English monoglot majority (and consequent resentment) because the new, bilingual Wales requires bilingual officers; but its long-term effects are likely to be disastrous for both communities.

Investiture, 1969 (1995). Cymru – Wales. The scene is Caernarfon, whose 'Golden Gate' was named after the one at Constantinople – see note to 'Caernarfon across brown fields' above.

Over the top (1995). The Welsh Language Society (Cymdeithas yr Iaith Gymraeg) organised demonstrations and non-violent resistance to Anglicization, often involving law-breaking, trouble with the police and criminal trials. The shock to respectable Welsh people was considerable as they saw teachers and ministers of religion, and their own sons and daughters, arrested and punished by the courts.

To ask for a bugle (1976). 'Poems of asking' are a recognised form in Welsh mediaeval bardic poetry. I also had in mind a poem by the twelfth-century master Cynddelw apostrophising the horn of Prince Llywelyn that was used like a bugle to summon his army to battle. Euros Bowen was a poet of great subtlety and nerve who achieved some notoriety at the time of the Investiture for what the press saw as support for terrorism.

Incomers (1998).

Bill of lading (1995). Country 133 – as a putative member of the United Nations.

Raymond Garlick (1995). Anglo-Welsh poet, editor and critic, a pacifist and erstwhile Roman Catholic and Welsh nationalist committed to the formation of a bilingual Welsh state as part of Europe and the United Nations. He and Roland Mathias founded *Dock Leaves*, later *The Anglo-Welsh Review*, which kept Anglo-Welsh literature alive in the dark years after the war; but in the early '60s moved out of Wales to teach in the Netherlands, returning in 1967 just as resistance to anglicisation was stiffening. The '70s were a time of struggle, even of bewilderment, for the poet; and they ended in disaster as his Welsh nationalism was hopelessly defeated in the 1979 Referendum on whether Wales should have a parliament.

In its phrasing, the poem echoes the English folksong 'The Lowlands of Holland'.

Referendum 1979 (1995). Ianws the Yank, the American-Welsh poet Jon Dressel, who lived near Garlick in Llanstephan. He collaborated with a Welsh-language poet in a hysterical sequence expressing their dismay during the week of the Referendum: it would have won the crown at the National

Eisteddfod (under the pen-name 'Ianws') but collaboration is against the rules. Raymond (Garlick) is called Cymro-Sais, i.e. Anglo-Welsh. O Conaráin is the original Irish form of my surname. Gruffydd the beak's son – Gruffydd ab yr Ynad Coch: see the poem and note about him earlier in this book. Owain in Sycharth – Owain Glyndŵr. John Tripp in Caerdydd (Cardiff), a nationalist and streetwise Anglo-Welsh poet.

Belle View (1993).

Caesar. Paudeens – little Paddies, Irishmen.

Elegy for the Welsh Dead, in the Falkland Islands, 1982 (1987). The poem is largely constructed round quotations from the *Book of Aneirin (Y Gododdin)*: see the note on 'Gwŷr a aeth Gatraeth' above. *Y Gododdin* names many of the warriors who went to take Catraeth and describes how brave they were. Many stanzas begin 'Men went to Catraeth'. The luxury of the liner that took the modern soldiers to the South Atlantic is compared with the feasting of the warband at Dun Eiddyn before the battle. 'Our boys' was how Mrs Thatcher used to refer to them. 'Though they went to church etc.' misquotes the line in *Y Gododdin*:

> Although they might go to shrines to do penance,
> This much was certain, death would transfix them.

In the third paragraph, Connah's Quay – in what is now Flintshire, the ancient Tegeingl (accented on the first syllable) or country of the Deceangli, a British tribe – was opposite the great Deeside steelworks, now closed, which gave employment to the whole area. You don't strictly 'pig' steel as far as I know – the term is used of an oblong mass of iron ('pig-iron') from a smelting furnace. Call it poetic license – the verb was too good to lose! 'The way of the wind and the rain was adamant' to an English reader recalls the refrain of the *Twelfth Night* song about

116

a man's growing up:

> When that I was but a tiny little boy,
>> With a heigh-ho, the wind and the rain

(and therefore makes a pun on Adam-ant); but to a Welsh reader it is a quotation from Gruffydd ab yr Ynad Coch's apocalyptic elegy on the conquest of Wales in 1282:

> See you not the way of the wind and the rain? . . .
> See you not the sun hurtling through the sky,
> And that the stars are fallen?

Pontypridd is in the South Wales mining valleys, so Clifford Elley 'was used to valleys' hence the reference to the twenty-third psalm:

> Yea, though I walk through the valley of the shadow of death, yet I will fear no evil; thy rod and thy staff comfort me. Thou hast prepared a table before me in the presence of my enemies. Thou annointest my head with oil.

The 'fasces' was a bundle of rods with an axe in the middle carried before a high magistrate in Rome. (The word 'fascist' comes from Mussolini's megalomaniac use of it as a badge to signify that his party would restore Roman glory to Italy: a fact not without relevance to my poem.) A tribune was an officer who represented the Roman plebs, as opposed to the patrician consul. Therefore, by analogy, a member of the House of Commons who represented us.

'Was he shy before girls?' like the warrior in *Gododdin* who was 'breathless before a girl, yet fierce in battle'. It is very important that I knew nothing about Phillip Sweet of Cwmbach. Even so I was uneasy of giving offence, and when I first published these lines I tried to disguise his identity.

'Russell Carlisle of Rhuthun' – Rhuthun (or Ruthin) is a town in north-east Wales. The whole valley between the Clwydian hills and the Denbighshire uplands is littered with castles – the one at Ruthin has been converted into a hotel. The name Carlisle, however, is from a town in the north-west of England, once part of the ancient British kingdom of Rheged, what the Welsh call the Old North. So in both senses the soldier was 'a man of the North', mourned by his compatriots.

'Uplifted hooves pawed at the lightning' – see the description of the war-horse in the *Book of Job*, Chapter 39, verses 19-25. 'With the dawn men went' – a quotation from *Y Gododdin*, used to introduce a number of stanzas. 'Gentlemen all' – I owe the word 'gentlemen' to the last section of David Jones's *In Parenthesis*, where the Queen of the Woods distributes her gifts to the dead soldiers:

> She speaks to them according to precedence. She knows what's due to this elect society. She can choose twelve gentle-men.

I call the Welsh soldiers 'dragons', partly because the flag of Cadwaladr, the legendary last king of Britain before the English conquest, was the Red Dragon. This was used by the Welshman Henry Tudor as his standard when he conquered England to become Henry VII. It then became the Welsh flag, so a 'dragon' is a 'kenning' or poetic nickname for a Welshman. But 'dragon' was also used by the Welsh poets to signify a great warrior, as in Gruffydd's elegy on the Edwardian conquest of Wales already mentioned.

Activist (1995). The *bro* (homeland or region) of summer stars was where Taliesin, the archetypal poet of Welsh legend, said he came from.

A square of grey slate (1987).

Wales (1995).

Pilgrim Way.

Ar y maes. See the next note.

Translation: *Between the Hosts.* A dream based on the opening of *The Bhagavad Gita* from the Indian epic *Mahaberata.* On the morning of battle in the civil war between his relatives, Arjuna the hero tells the god Krishna, who is his charioteer, to drive into no-man's-land between the armies so that he can survey the two sides; and he falls into despair at the prospect of killing his kinsfolk.

In my dream the two sides are, first, the adherents of Wales as a separate country – Llywelyn the Last Prince, and his poet Gruffydd ab yr Ynad Coch; Owain Glyndŵr; T. Gwynn Jones, the early twentieth-century poet of *Madog*; Saunders Lewis the founder of Plaid Cymru; Waldo Williams the quaker poet; Gwynfor Evans the first Plaid Cymru M.P.; and the Anglo-Welsh poets, R.S. Thomas, Harri Webb (editor of *The Welsh Nation*) and John Tripp.

And second, those who have from the fall of Rome onwards hankered for, or been content with, a revival of Britain, with the Welsh as founder-members of the new empire – Brân the mythological king in the *Mabinogion*; Macsen the Roman emperor (Maximus) who in legend married a girl from Caernarfon on the Seiont; Hywel of the Axe, a Welsh follower of Edward III and castellan of Harlech praised by Iolo Goch; Dafydd ap Gwilym the love-poet; Guto'r Glyn whose finest poems were written when he was old and blind; the socialists Keir Hardie (M.P. for Aberdare) and Aneurin Bevan; together with my own family and the Anglo-Welsh poet, Dylan Thomas.